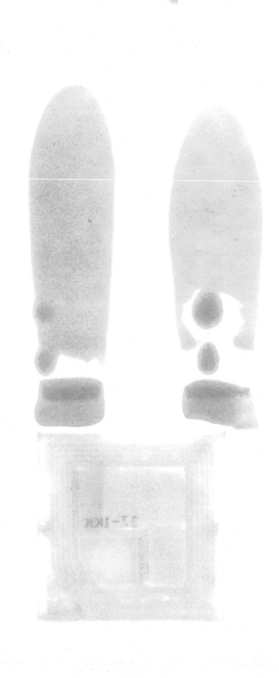

People of the Bible

The Bible through stories and pictures

Abraham and Isaac

Copyright © in this format Belitha Press Ltd., 1985

Text copyright © Catherine Storr 1985

Illustrations copyright © Gavin Rowe 1985

Art Director: Treld Bicknell

First published in the United States of America 1985
by Raintree Publishers Inc.
330 East Kilbourn Avenue, Milwaukee, Wisconsin 53202
in association with Belitha Press Ltd., London.

Conceived, designed and produced by Belitha Press Ltd.,
2 Beresford Terrace, London N5 2DH

ISBN 0-8172-1994-3 (U.S.A.)

Library of Congress Cataloging in Publication Data

Storr, Catherine.
    Abraham and Isaac.

    (People of the Bible)
    Summary: Relates the story of Abraham's fidelity to
God and love for his son Isaac.
      1. Abraham (Biblical patriarch)—Juvenile literature.
2. Isaac (Biblical patriarch)—Juvenile literature.
3. Patriarchs (Bible)—Biography—Juvenile literature.
4. Bible O.T.—Biography—Juvenile literature.
[1. Abraham (Biblical patriarch) 2. Isaac (Biblical
patriarch) 3. Bible stories—O.T.] I. Title. II. Series.
BS573.S84   1984   222′.110922   84-18076

ISBN 0-8172-1994-3

First published in Great Britain 1985
by Franklin Watts Ltd.,
12a Golden Square, London W1

Printed in Hong Kong by South China Printing Co.

234567890   89 88 87 86 85

Abraham and Isaac

Retold by Catherine Storr
Pictures by Gavin Rowe

Raintree Childrens Books
Milwaukee • Toronto • Melbourne • London
Belitha Press Limited • London

In the city of Haran lived a man called Abraham. His wife was called Sarah.

One day Abraham heard God speaking to him. "You must leave your father's house and his family. I will show you a land where you and your children and your children's children shall live."

Abraham took Sarah and his nephew, Lot, and everything they possessed, and they journeyed to the south, to the land of Canaan.

When they arrived, God spoke to Abraham again. "This is the land where you, and your children, and your children's children will live." But Abraham said, "Lord God, I have no children of my own to inherit this land." God said, "Go to the door of the tent and look up at the night sky. Can you count the stars? Your children's children will be as many as that."

In the middle of a hot day, Abraham was sitting at the door of his tent. He looked up and saw three strangers standing near him. He knew that they were not just ordinary men, so he bowed himself to the ground.

He said, "Don't go away. Come into my tent and let me wash your feet, and while you rest, I will find a morsel of bread for you to eat." Then he hurried to find Sarah. "Quickly, make some cakes," he said, "while I get a young calf for a feast." He fetched milk and butter and set out the feast under a tree, and the three strangers ate.

10

The strangers said to Abraham, "Where is Sarah, your wife?"

"She is in the tent," Abraham said.

"She is going to have a son," the strangers said.

Sarah was behind the door of the tent. When she heard this, she laughed. "I am much too old to have a baby son," she thought.

The strangers heard her laughing and said to Abraham, "Why did Sarah laugh? Doesn't she know that God can do anything, however hard it is?"

Abraham went with the strangers to the city of Sodom. There he heard the voice of God. "The people of Sodom are very wicked," God said. "I am going to destroy the city."

"Lord, will you destroy the good people as well as the bad? If there are fifty good people, won't you spare the city?"

God said, "If there are fifty good people, I will spare the city." Then Abraham asked God to spare the city for the sake of forty, or for thirty or twenty men. At last God said, "Even if there are only ten good people, I will not destroy Sodom."

That evening, God sent two angels to visit Sodom. Lot was sitting at the gate of the city. He went to meet the angels, and he took them into his house.

The wicked people of Sodom came to Lot's house and said, "Send these men out into the street." They tried to break down the door of the house to reach the two angels. But God struck them all blind.

The angels said to Lot, "Make haste! Take your wife and your daughters, and leave this city before God destroys it." They took Lot and his wife and his daughters and led them out of the city.

"Escape for your life and go up into the mountains," they said. "But you must not look back at the city in the plain." Lot and his family escaped up to the hills.

But Lot's wife turned to look back. As she did, God turned her into a pillar of salt.

Some time later, God kept his promise to Abraham and Sarah. Sarah had a baby son. Sarah and Abraham rejoiced and thanked God for giving them a son in their old age.

They called the baby Isaac, and they loved him very much. He grew to be a young lad, and brought his mother and father great joy.

But one day God wanted to test Abraham's faith. He called, "Abraham!" Abraham said, "I am here, Lord." God said, "Take your son, your only son, Isaac, up into the mountains and offer him there as a burnt sacrifice." Abraham was very sad. But he felt that he must do what God told him.

So he rose early the next morning and saddled his donkey.

Abraham took Isaac, his son, and two young
men, and the wood for the burnt offering.
They traveled toward the mountains.

21

After they had traveled for three days, Abraham said to the two young men, "You stay here with the donkey! I and the lad will go up the mountain by ourselves." Abraham took the knife, and Isaac carried the wood for the fire.

Isaac said, "Father!"

"What is it, my son?"

"Here is the wood and the fire for the burnt offering. Where is the lamb to sacrifice?"

Abraham said, "God will provide the lamb, my son."

When they reached the top of the mountain, Abraham built the altar. He laid Isaac on it and took the knife in his hand, ready to sacrifice his only son.

Just as he was raising the knife to strike, he heard the voice of God again. "Abraham! Abraham! Don't lay a hand on Isaac. Now I know that you trust me and will obey me. Look in the thicket."

Abraham looked, and there he saw a ram caught in the thicket. He lifted Isaac off the altar, and he offered up the ram as a sacrifice instead of his son.

Time passed, and Sarah died. Abraham
thought that now he should find a wife for
Isaac. He wanted Isaac to marry a girl from his
own country.

He sent his servant to that place and told
him to find a girl from his own people, who
would come to Canaan to marry Isaac.

The servant took camels and jewels and gifts. When he came to a well, near the city of Nabor, he prayed, "Lord God of my master, I shall ask all the girls coming to the well to give me water. I pray you, let the girl I have come to find answer, 'I will draw water for your camels also.'"

Before he had finished praying, a girl came out of the city and came to the well. Abraham's servant said to her, "I pray you, let me drink a little water from your pitcher."

The girl said, "Drink, my lord."

She let down her pitcher into the well, and first she gave water to the servant. Then she said, "I will draw water for your camels, too." Then the servant gave her a gold earring and two golden bracelets.

He asked, "Whose daughter are you?"

"I am Rebecca, daughter of Bethnel. Come back with me to my father's house. We have room for you and for your camels."

When he heard these words, Abraham's servant knew that he had found the right wife for Isaac, his master's son. He went with Rebecca to the house of her brother, Laban. Laban said, "God has sent you here."

So Rebecca went back to Canaan with Abraham's servant, to marry Isaac.

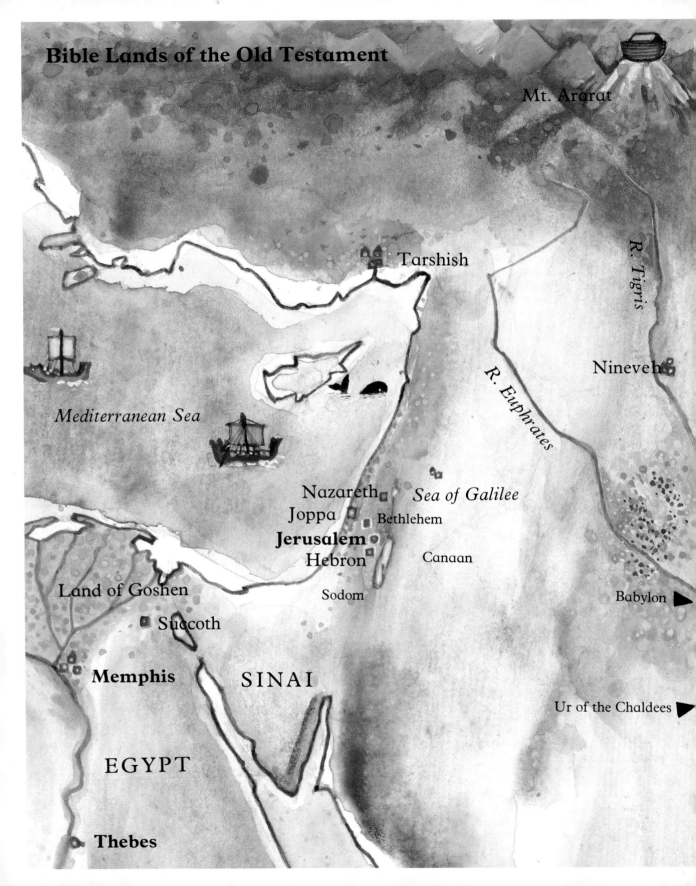

Bible Lands of the Old Testament

Mt. Ararat

Tarshish

R. Tigris

Nineveh

Mediterranean Sea

R. Euphrates

Nazareth

Sea of Galilee

Joppa

Bethlehem

Jerusalem

Hebron

Canaan

Sodom

Babylon ◄

Land of Goshen

Succoth

Ur of the Chaldees ◄

Memphis

SINAI

EGYPT

Thebes